First Facts®

Earn It, Save It, Spend It!

Donate Money

by Emily Raij

PEBBLE
a capstone imprint

First Facts are published by Pebble
1710 Roe Crest Drive, North Mankato, Minnesota 56003
www.mycapstone.com

Library of Congress Cataloging-in-Publication Data
Names: Raij, Emily, author.
Title: Donate money / by Emily Raij.
Description: North Mankato, Minnesota : Pebble, [2020] | Series: First facts.
  Earn it, save it, spend it!
Identifiers: LCCN 2018060561| ISBN 9781977108340 (hardcover) |
  ISBN 9781977110053 (pbk.) | ISBN 9781977108548 (ebook pdf)
Subjects: LCSH: Money—Juvenile literature. | Charities—Juvenile literature.
Classification: LCC HG221.5 .R35 2019 | DDC 361.7/4—dc23
LC record available at https://lccn.loc.gov/2018060561

Editorial Credits
Karen Aleo, editor; Sarah Bennett, designer; Tracy Cummins, media researcher;
Kathy McColley, production specialist

Photo Credits
Capstone Studio: Karon Dubke, Back Cover, Design Element; Denise Mackinnon: 9
Right; Emily Raij: 9 Left; iStockphoto: AfricaImages, 21, David Sacks, 15, fstop123,
13, Steve Debenport, 11; Shutterstock: jakkapan, Design Element, Kaikoro, 5,
Monika Chodak, 17 Bottom, New Africa, 7, Nik Merkulov, Design Element, Pashin
Georgiy, 17 Top, Rido, 19, Thomas J. Sebourn, Cover, vipman, Design Element

All internet sites appearing in back matter were available and accurate when this
book was sent to press.

Printed and bound in China.
1671

Table of Contents

CHAPTER 1

Ways to Donate

Have you ever wondered how you can help others? Some people give money to others who need it. The money is a gift. It does not need to be paid back. Other people **donate** their time or money to **charities**. Charities are groups that help people in need.

FACT

All people have basic needs. Basic needs are food, clothing, and housing. Many charities help others meet these needs.

donate—to help by giving money, time, or something as a gift

charity—a group that raises money or collects goods to help people in need

Charities collect food, clothing, and other items for people in need. They collect items for animals in need too. Charities also collect money to buy these items. People make these donations. Some people donate **goods** they already have. These goods might include used clothing, blankets, or canned food.

FACT

When donating used clothing, make sure it is clean and free of holes. Clothes and shoes should be in good enough shape to wear.

goods—things or belongings, such as food, clothing, or toys

Charities can raise money for a **cause** like education and curing diseases. Charities often sell items to raise money too. The money goes to a good cause.

A Good Cause

Teach for America is a group that helps train new teachers. They also assign teachers to schools. Teach for America sold tickets to a big dinner party. The event raised money to train new teachers.

cause—an aim or principle for which people believe in and work

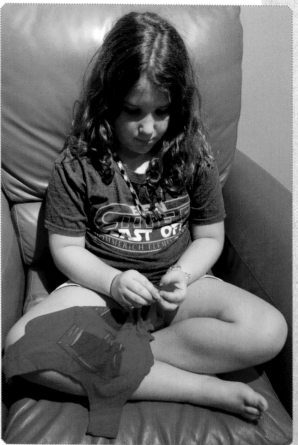

People can also raise money. Two students sold handmade bookmarks and bags. The girls donated the money to their school. That money helped pay for a school garden.

CHAPTER 2

Why Do People Donate?

What makes people want to donate? Many people want to help make their **community** a better place. There are also lots of rewards from donating. People learn about **cooperation** when working together. Being helpful is fun and feels good too!

community—a group of people who live in the same area

cooperation—working with other people to do a good job

People also **volunteer** to solve a problem. They might collect food and supplies for a community hit by a hurricane. They may raise money for new books or computers at a local school.

The Red Cross

When a natural disaster happens, the Red Cross is there to help out. The Red Cross is an **organization** that raises money. The money is used to help people. This money helps pay for things, such as housing, food, and first aid.

volunteer—to offer to do something without pay

organization—people joined together for a certain purpose

Many people volunteer because of an interest they have. Someone who is good at math might volunteer to tutor children who need help learning math.

CHAPTER 3

Try It!

Is there a charity you would like to donate money to? You can have a yard sale! Start by collecting the things you no longer use. If you like to make art, you can sell your work. With an adult's help, sell these items at the sale. Then donate the money to a charity.

Make a flyer about your yard sale. Be sure to list the date, time, and place. Describe the charity you are raising money for and what it does. Add what you are selling or how people can contact you to learn more.

FACT
Spread the word! Ask your teacher if you can pass out your flyers at school. Check if you can place signs at local libraries and bookstores too.

Shop for crafts and a cause at our yard sale!

We are raising money for American Humane!
They look after the safety and care of animals.

Saturday, September 15

1234 Arbor Lane

1–3 p.m.

If a yard sale is not for you, that is OK. Think about a charity you'd like to help. Then think about how much money you want to raise. Invite friends and family to help. Make a **plan** for reaching your **goals**. Include the due date for raising money and the steps to take each week.

> **FACT**
> Raising money teaches you how to be a leader. You can make decisions and help a team work together to reach a goal.

plan—a decision for how something will be done

goal—something that you aim for or work toward

Talk to your parents about the charities they help or donate to. Do you want to help those groups too? Or do you want to help solve another problem?

Donating time or money makes a difference and brings people together. It feels good to give. And that is a real gift!

Glossary

cause (KAWZ)—an aim or principle for which people believe in and work

charity (CHAYR-uh-tee)—a group that raises money or collects goods to help people in need

community (kuh-MYOO-nuh-tee)—a group of people who live in the same area

cooperation (koh-op-uh-RAY-shuhn)—working together to do a good job

donate (DOH-nayt)—to help by giving money, time, or something as a gift

goal (GOHL)—something that you aim for or work toward

goods (GUDZ)—things or belongings, such as food, clothing, or toys

organization (or-guh-nuh-ZAY-shuhn)—people joined together for a certain purpose

plan (PLAN)—a decision for how something will be done

volunteer (vol-uhn-TIHR)—to offer to do something without pay

Read More

Ancona, George. *Can We Help? Kids Volunteering to Help Their Communities.* Somerville, MA: Candlewick Press, 2015.

Colby, Jennifer. *Donating.* My Guide to Money. Ann Arbor, MI: Cherry Lake Publishing, 2018.

Schuh, Mari. *Save, Spend, or Share.* Money and Me. Vero Beach, FL: Rourke Educational Media, 2018.

Internet Sites

KidsHealth: Be a Volunteer
https://kidshealth.org/en/kids/volunteering.html

Youth Service America: Youth Changing the World
https://leadasap.ysa.org/wp-content/uploads/2017/10/English-Youth-Changing-the-World-Toolkit.pdf

Critical Thinking Questions

1. What are some ways you can help others?

2. What are some reasons people donate?

3. Think of how you can donate money. What are your ideas?

Index